This book belongs to
_____

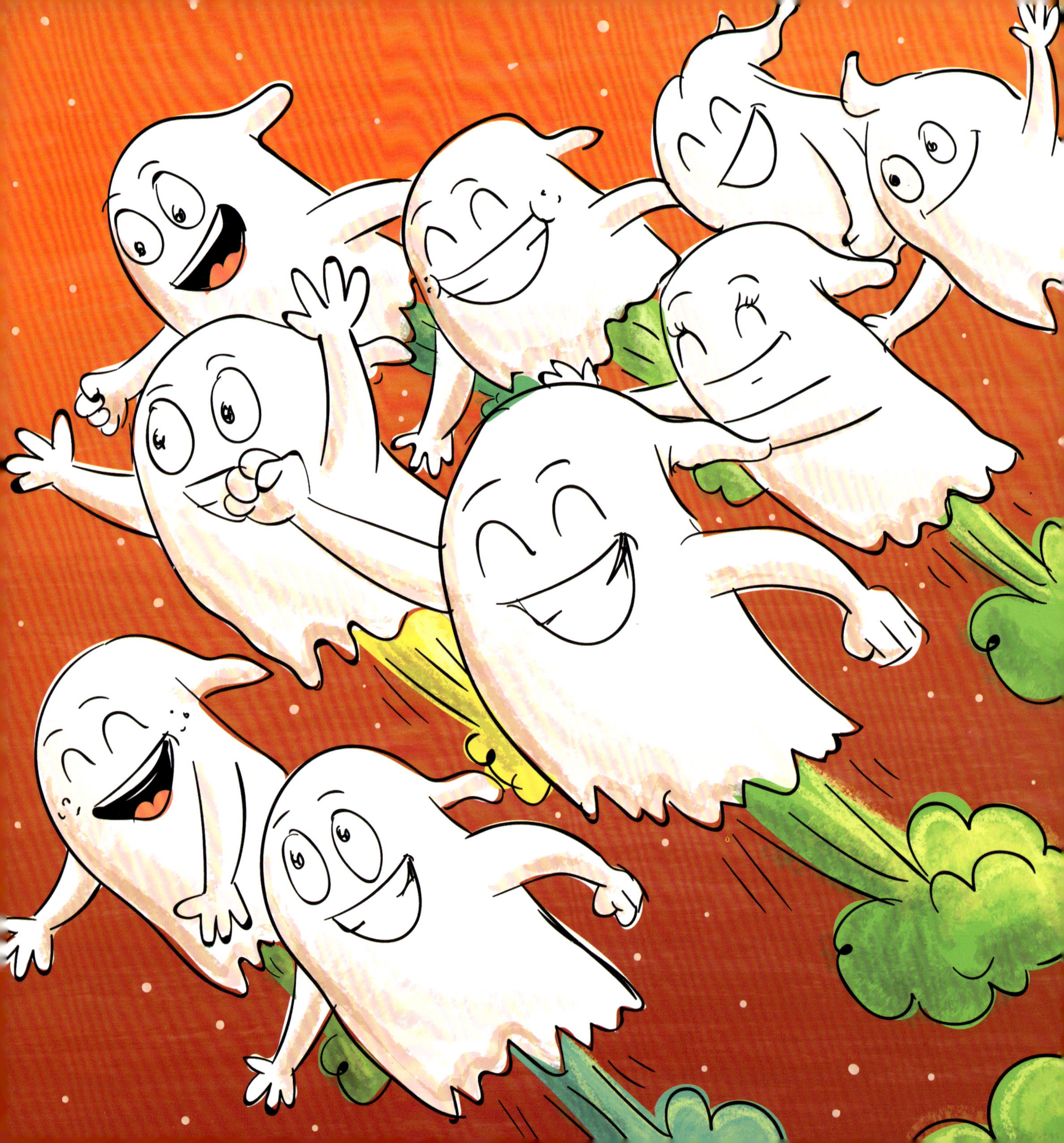

Copyright © 2022 Humor Heals Us. All rights reserved. No part of this book may be reproduced in any form without permission in writing from the publisher. Please send bulk order requests to Humorhealsus@gmail.com Printed and bound in the USA. humorhealsus.com

Paperback ISBN: 978-1-63731-426-5
Hardcover ISBN: 978-1-63731-428-9

10 Gassy Ghosts

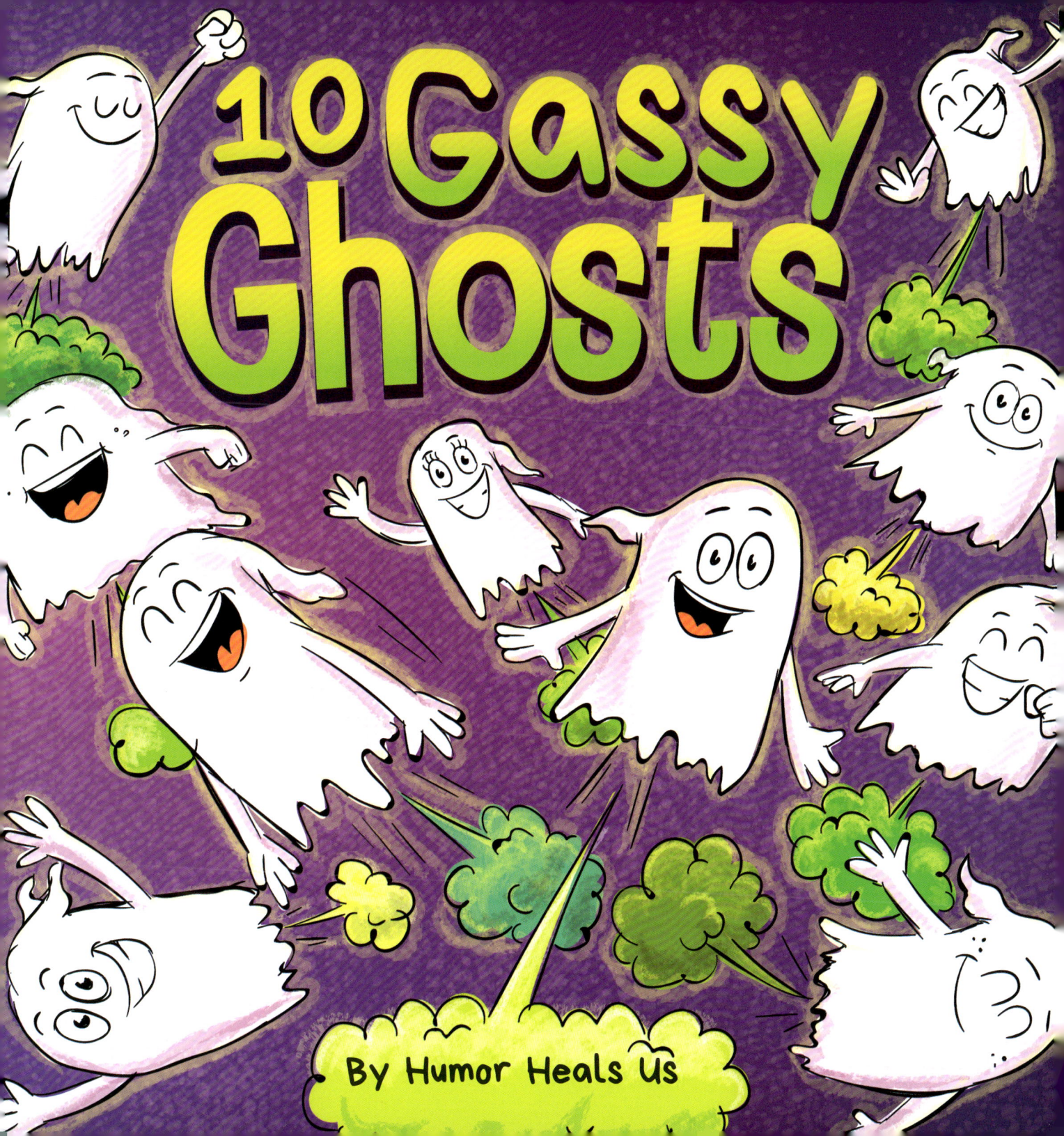

By Humor Heals Us

The moon shined brightly
Although the sky was dark.
All was quiet and still
Across the SpooKey park.

High up in the tree,
Where the wind seemed to howl most,
Were 10 stinky, smelly,
Very **GASSY** Ghosts!

Ghost **1** seemed to toot
Every time he would float!
Wouldn't you believe it,
His gas really **STUNK** for a ghost!

He didn't eat real food.
So you would think surely
That a ghost like Ghost 1
Would not be very **STINKY**.

Ghost **2** and Ghost **3** had a different gas
That was especially **LOUD**.
And when they'd let out a toot,
You better believe they were proud!

Sometimes their gas could be heard for miles.
All throughout the town,
The noise would send vibrations
That could be heard all around.

SpooKey Park
5 miles

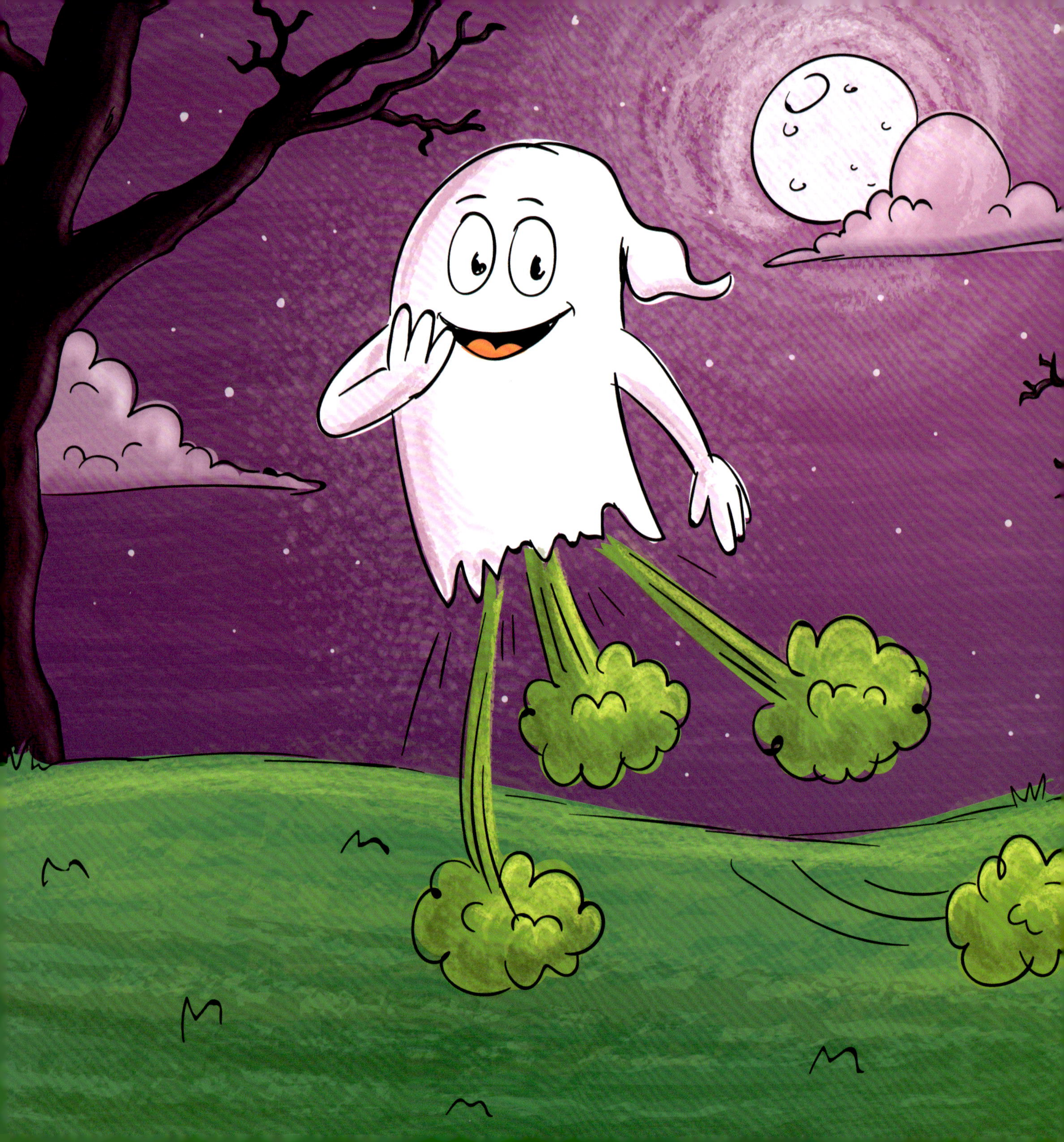

Ghost 4 let out little poots
That sounded kind of squeaky.
The high-pitched noises were even
Considered to be a little creepy.

Ghost **5** had gas that sounded lowwww,
Like a thunderous kind of bass.
The kind that would make your lips flap
If they smacked you in the face.

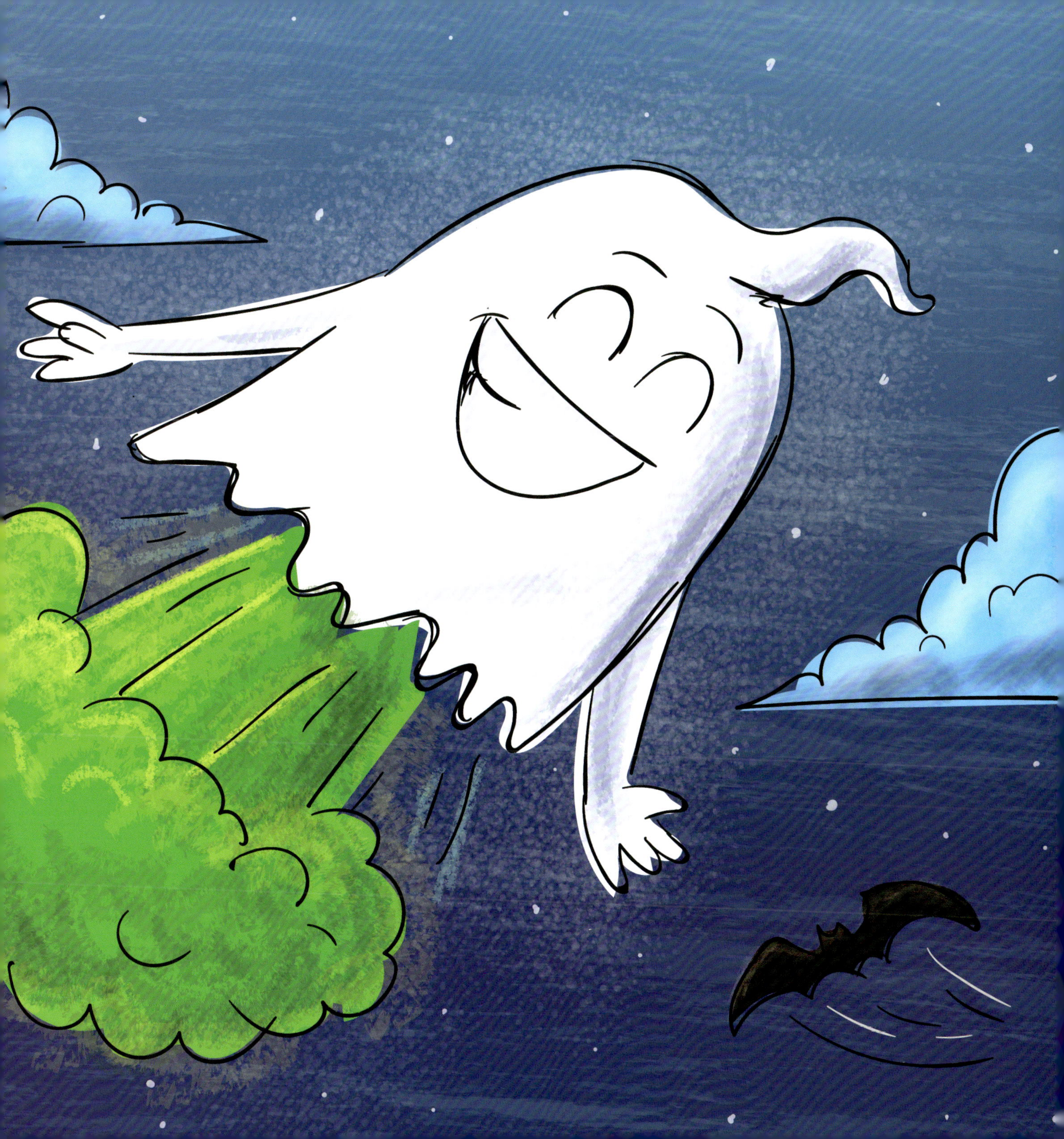

Ghost **6** felt a little silly
When he had to let one out.
Ghost **7** proudly blasted them off
Without a second doubt.

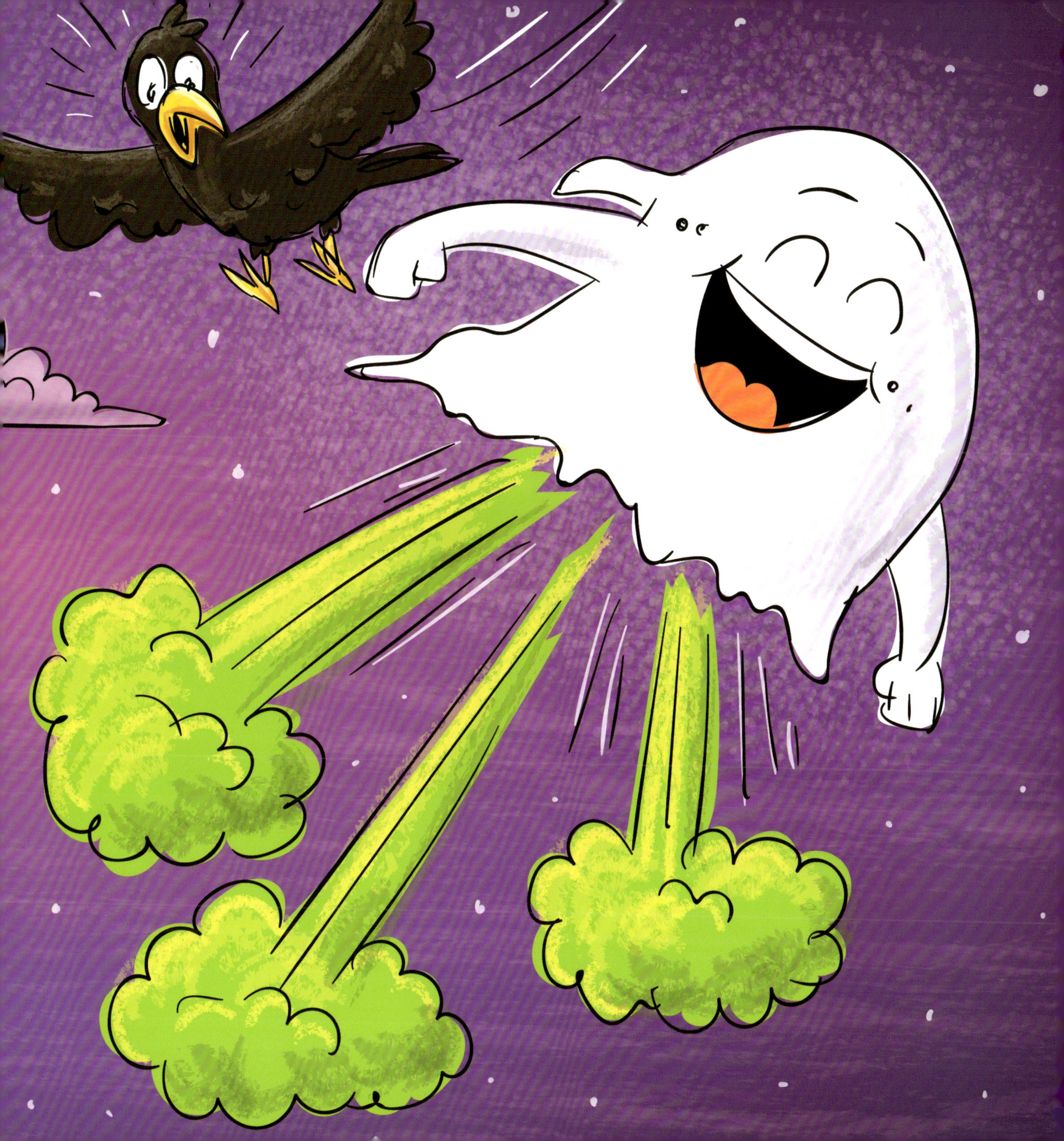

Ghost 8 let out silent ones
With a stench that would ruin plants.
Sometimes the smell was so toxic
It would even kill the ants.

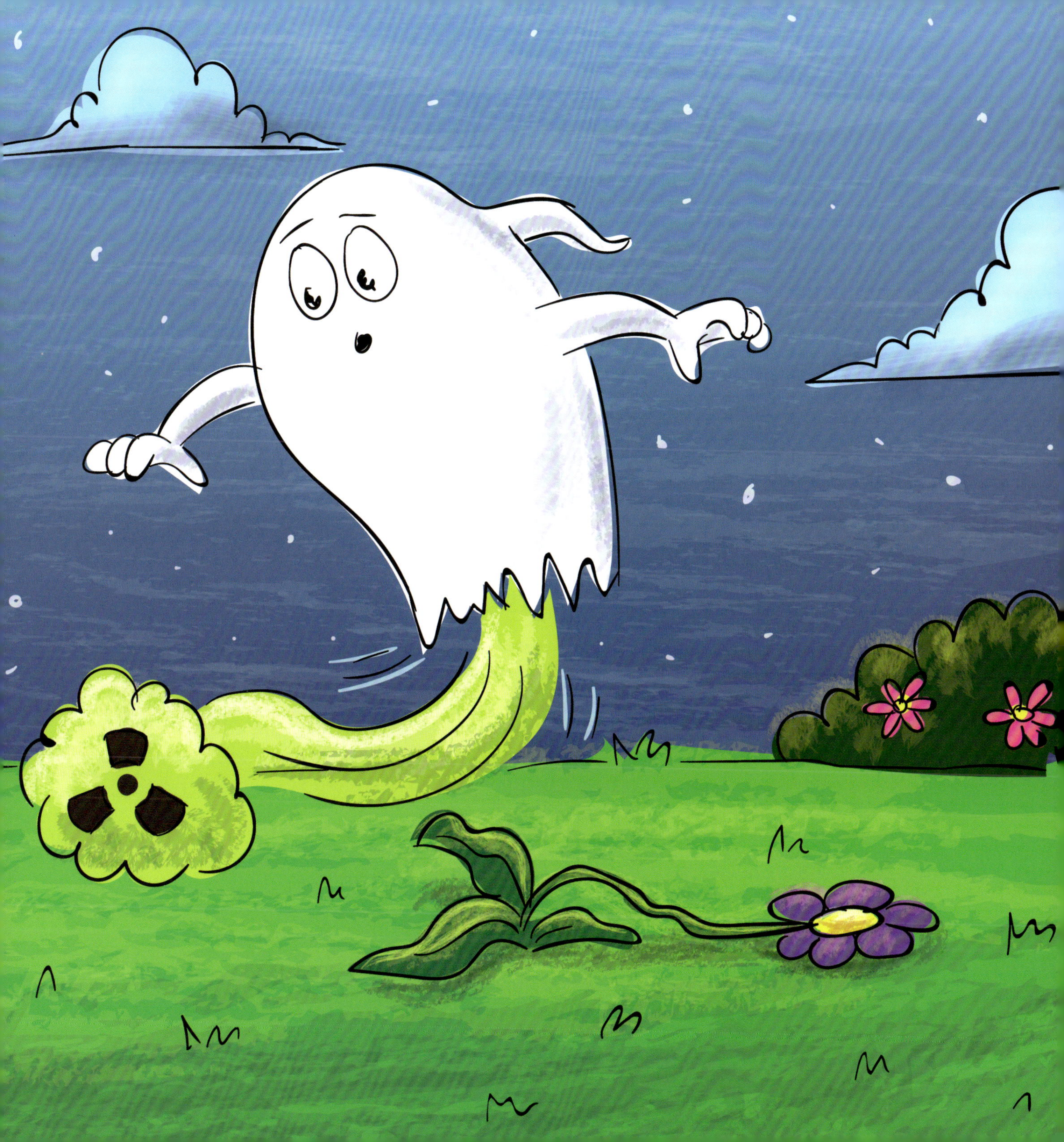

Ghost 9, her toots were majestic,
Almost what dreams were made of.
They would linger on for hours
And leave a cloud-like dust up above.

Her gas was visible to anyone near
But also from afar,
It glimmered and glittered in the night sky
As if it was made up of stars.

But the smelliest, loudest, scariest gas
Came from Ghost **10**.
Even if you didn't see the ghost,
Through his gas, you'd know where he'd been.

No other ghost or being
Could produce gas half as smelly.
Every time he tooted
You knew something was **ROTTEN** in his belly.

On this night, the ghosts went out.
It was time for them to haunt,
But Ghost **10**, he just wasn't
In the mood for a midnight jaunt.

"I think I'll stay behind," he said.
"You go on, enjoy the night."
And the 9 other ghosts set out
To scare the town with fright.

Ghost **10** decided to wait
And perch in the tallest tree.
He glided along the trunk
Yelling, "**WHOOPEE!**"

He was zipping up so fast,
He didn't notice a big spider web.
And in front of him a big spider
With 8 dangly, spiky legs.

"I'm going to **EAT YOU**!" the spider said to
Scared and crying little Ghost 10.
The ghost writhed and wiggled
To get out of the web, and **THEN**...

HE LET OUT HIS GHOSTLY GAS!

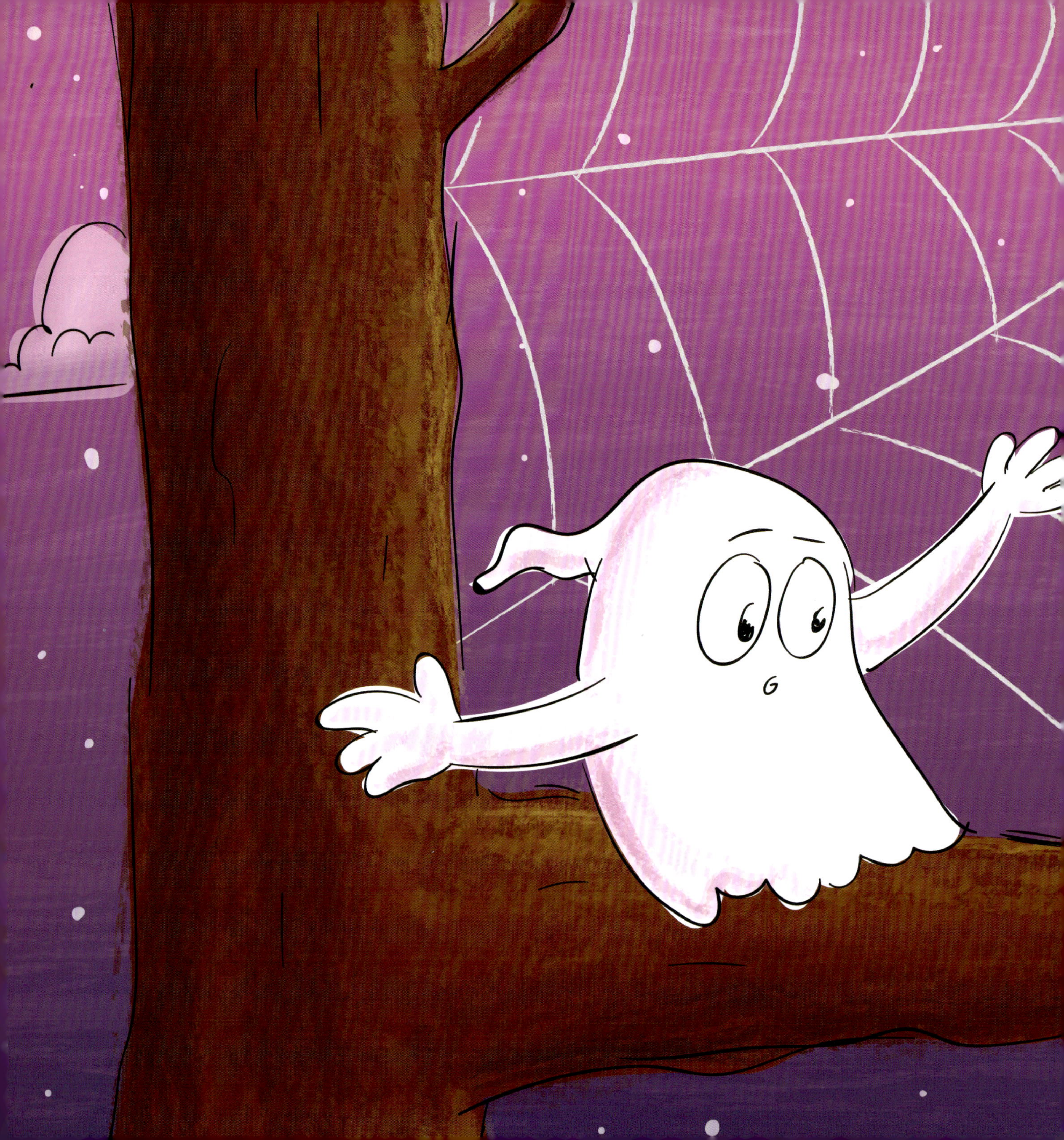

The spider instantly passed out
And fell swiftly to the ground,
As the gas of tiny Ghost **10**
Let out a booming sound!

Soon all the other ghosts arrived.
One said, "Ghost **10**! We heard your gas!"
And the ghosts worked together to free Ghost **10**
Before much time had passed.

So in the end, the ghost with the smelliest toots,
The grossest of them all,
Was the ghost whose stinky gas
Also doubled as a call.

Ghost **10** was super glad
For his gassiness in the end.
But more than that,
Ghost **10** was so grateful for his friends.

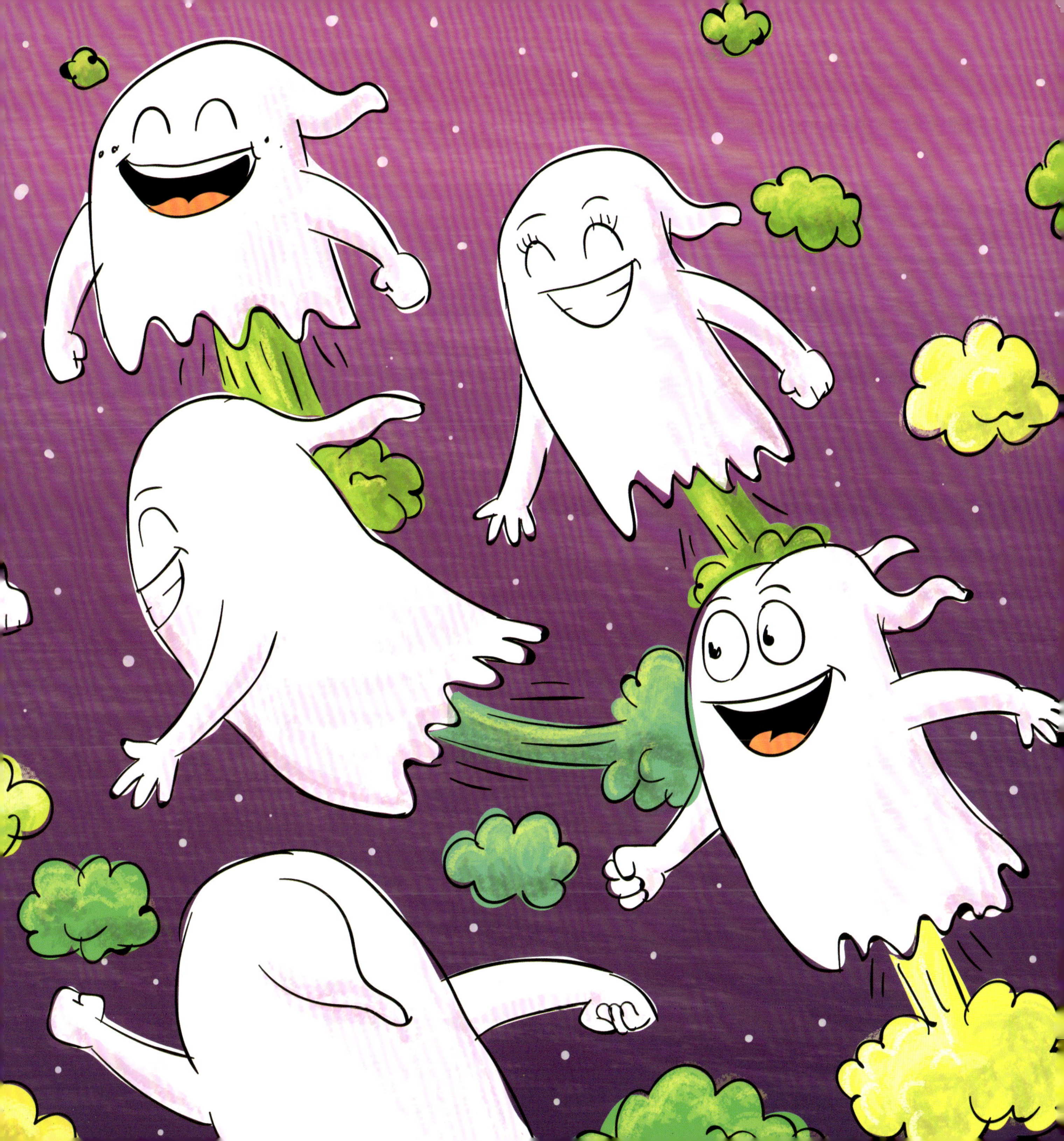

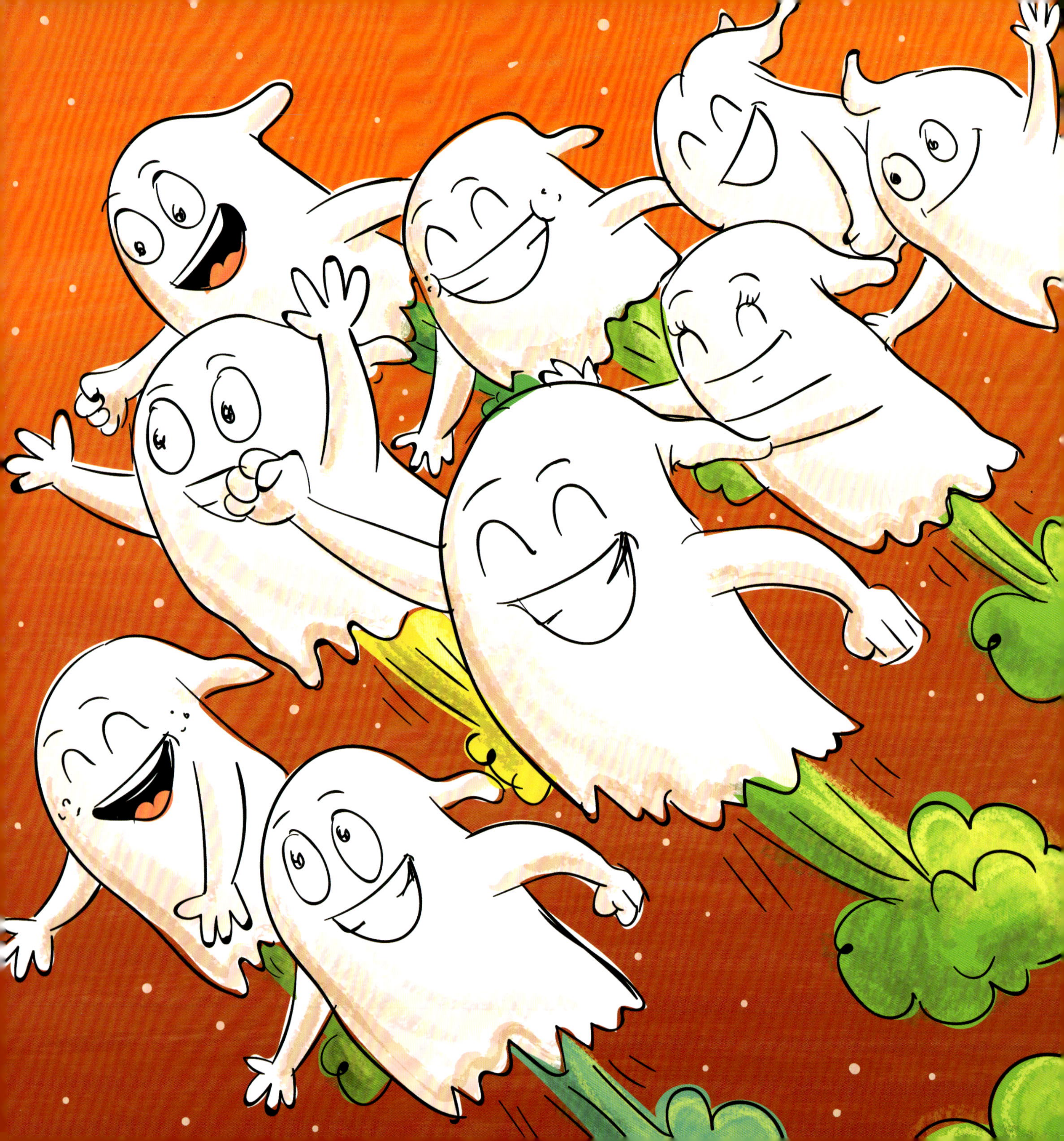